Updated 2024

The Untainted Egyptian Origin

Why Ancient Egypt Matters

Moustafa Gadalla

CONTENTS

1

ABOUT THE AUTHOR

Moustafa Gadalla is an Egyptian-American independent Egyp-tologist who was born in Cairo, Egypt in 1944. He holds a Bache-lor of Science degree in civil engineering from Cairo University.

From his early childhood, Gadalla pursued his Ancient Egyptian roots with passion, through continuous study and research. Since 1990, he has dedicated and concentrated all his time to researching and writing.

Gadalla is the author of twenty-two published internationally acclaimed books about the various aspects of the Ancient Egypt-ian history and civilization and its influences worldwide. In addition he operates a multimedia resource center for accurate, educative studies of Ancient Egypt, presented in an engaging, practical, and interesting manner that appeals to the general pub-lic.

He was the Founder of Tehuti Research Foundation which was later incorporated into the multi-lingual Egyptian Wisdom Center (https://www.egyptianwisdomcenter.org) in more than ten languages. The website also includes another ongoing activity which includes his creation and production of performing arts projects such as the Isis Rises Operetta, Horus The Initiate Operetta; Egyptian Goddesses Operetta; and a few more other productions to follow.

2

FORWARD BY PAUL JEFFELS

Throughout the ancient world, right up until almost the fall of the Roman Empire, Egypt was regarded as the cradle of civilization. The Christians and Muslims made strenuous efforts through the Dark Ages and the Medieval Period to eradicate the cultural legacy of Egypt. Their principle weapon was to forbid the knowledge of Egyptian writing and language.

However, so many Greek and Roman accounts of the glories of Egypt survived in classical writings that these misguided efforts only served to increase interest among philosophical circles, and to create an aura of mystery and forbidden fruit around Egyptian wisdom and culture.

This was increased by the reputation, in classical writing, of Egypt as the land of magic, and the numerous references to Egypt made in the Christian Bible.

Furthermore, in philosophical circles, there were numerous references to the 'Hermetic Texts'. Until the 16th century, only Latin versions of parts of these texts existed. By the 16th century, scholars had been searching for the complete texts for 1,000 years. When the Greek versions of almost all of the texts turned up, they caused a sensation and had a major influence on the Renaissance.

The Hermetic Texts are Egyptian wisdom with a Greek overlay, written (probably) in Alexandria around 200 CE. By the 17th century, they were regarded as frauds. When the esoteric aspects of Egyptian writing were translated in the 19th century, it became apparent that a strong Egyptian element was contained in these texts, and thus began a process of re-evaluating the influence of Egyptian culture and wisdom on modern society and thought.

Civilized Values

Egyptian culture was based on Maat—the rightness of the Universe. Maat could be described as 'that which supports the Principle of Being'. Egyptians believed in an animated universe in which the Principle of Being was the most manifest aspect of the One Great God. Consequently, they constructed their society on the basis of working Maat—supporting the Principle of Being.

To this end, they were the first culture to abolish human sacrifice and to enshrine in law the notion that every human being has the right to life. This meant that murder and violent crimes against the individual attracted severe punishment, and the State could only punish people after a due process of law had taken place. Every culture and civilization that has endured for any length of time has adopted this principle, demonstrating that it is truly fundamental knowledge about the fabric of the Universe.

It is the basis of the US Constitution and the UN Charter.

Working through the implications of this core principle, lawmakers reasoned that in order to support life, people need food, accommodation, possessions, and clearly defined relationships with other people. All of these became enshrined in Egyptian law.

The Organization of Thought

By observing reality, the Egyptians noted that Maat generally worked through repeating patterns. So they set out to observe these patterns and find ways of working with them. They soon realized that this requires systems to measure and quantify, partly in order to measure and control and partly to prevent the human mind from wandering off into beliefs about reality that deviated from what was actually there. Consequently, they invented a coherent system of writing, enabling the keeping of long-term records, a coherent mathematical system, and an effective system of weights and measures, enabling them to quantify effectively.

The Egyptian system of mathematics was still being used for practical purposes, such as land surveying, right into the Middle Ages, as Greek theoretical mathematics was useless for this purpose.

The Organization of the State

Geographically, the Egyptian state was the largest in the Ancient world, before the Assyrian empire. It certainly lasted the longest—longer than any other state in recorded history. In part, this was because the Egyptians invented the concepts of state-employed public servants and an independent judiciary. One issue that drove this was the annual flood of the Nile. Every year those areas likely to flood were surveyed and the results recorded in triplicate. After the flood subsided, these areas were surveyed again, and all boundaries and properties were reinstated. The results were recorded in triplicate again, ready for the whole process to be repeated next year. This system was enshrined in Egyptian law, which itself was probably the most just and incorruptible system that has ever been devised.

Egyptian law was administered by state-appointed judges, each of whom was dedicated to the pursuit and maintenance of Maat in her aspect of absolute truth. To this end, all eloquence was banned from legal proceedings. All submissions by both prosecution and defense had to be made in writing. The judges took these statements and then left the courtroom to consider them objectively before making a judgment. We could do with a system like that today!

Science and Medicine

Egyptian science and medicine was based entirely on the practical principle of improving life for people. It operated entirely within the moral considerations of Maat. Nothing was done or experimented with that disobeyed this principle. We could do with this today, a point that has been made by many modern scientists, including Albert Einstein and Robert Oppenheimer—both associated with the invention of atomic weapons.

The Greeks acknowledged that their medical knowledge came from Egypt. Documentary and archaeological evidence confirms that the Egyptians could effectively treat broken bones, flesh wounds, and even skull fractures. This is largely because the Egyptians were the first people to recognize the connection between cleanliness and health. Cleanliness meant that invasive surgical procedures could be carried out effectively, and the population was much less subject to epidemics. It is estimated that at the height of the New Kingdom, around 1300 BCE, the population of Egypt was 7 million. In 1800, after centuries of Islamic occupation, it was only 3 million.

Documentary evidence, both from Egyptian sources and other civilized countries, tells us that the Egyptians were very successful in treating psychological disorders. In fact, they were considered the world leaders; an aspect that derived from their intense studies of the organization of the mind and the means of controlling it.

Technology, Art, Craft, and Agriculture

Any person who has seen Egyptian artifacts close up will have been impressed by the excellence of both their design and workmanship. This ethos of practical perfection was created by the fact that Egyptians saw no separation between the spiritual and the mundane. Every artifact served both its immediate purpose and the work of the Universe in nurturing and supporting Being. The shapes of hand tools, for instance, are prototypes for the hand tools we use today. Furniture and jewelry identical to Egyptian designs can be found in modern high street stores. Many a recipe served in modern homes and restaurants graced the tables of the Egyptians 4,000 years ago.

The jewel in the crown of Egyptian technology was their mastery of irrigation and flood management. In many parts of Egypt, irrigation canals that were dug in 2500 BCE still serve their original purpose. All irrigation systems used today are based on systems devised by the Egyptians. It was this organized agriculture that enabled the Egyptian state to support its huge population and still have sufficient resources to create the civilization that we admire today.

Conclusion

Ancient Egypt was the cradle of our modern Western civilization/culture. Every technology and system we have today was prefigured in Egypt by 2500 BCE. But we still have more to learn from Egypt. What we have lost is the understanding that every action must be directed towards the greater good—in Egyptian terms, the support of Maat, which (in the terms I have used) means support of the Principle of Being. If the human race would discipline itself to do this, we could eliminate war, famine, and almost all crime within a few years. This was the belief of the visionaries who wrote the United Nations charter 70 years ago after the most destructive war in human history. That belief started in Ancient Egypt and has continued to inspire progressive thinkers through the dark years since the civilization of Egypt was destroyed by invaders.

We would do well to look again at the beliefs of Ancient Egypt and their long-term success in applying them, learn the lessons, and apply those understandings and positive beliefs to our own lives and the modern world in general.

Paul Jeffels
Board Member of Tehuti Research Foundation

3

PREFACE

This book is intended to provide a short introductory overview of some aspects of the Ancient Egyptian civilization that can serve us well nowadays in our daily lives no matter where we are in this world.

Topics presented cover:

– Our place in the universe and its operational system.

– Understanding oneself and how to sort out internal energies to live happy and healthy.

– Problems and old [Egyptian] remedies of political, social and economical conditions.

– How to achieve peaceful coexistence between peoples, lands and natural resources; which also deals with having a clean environment.

– Understanding and implementing harmonic principles into building construction.

– Appreciation of art and its functions and applications in a harmonic fashion.

– The timeless nature of the Ancient Egyptian civilization.

Moustafa Gadalla
Author

4

STANDARDS AND TERMINOLOGY

---

1. The Ancient Egyptian word neter and its feminine form netert have been wrongly, and possibly intentionally, translated to *god* and *goddess*, by almost all academicians. Neteru (plural of neter/netert) are the divine principles and functions of the One Supreme God.

2. You may find variations in writing the same Ancient Egyptian term, such as Amen/Amon /Amun or Pir/Per. This is because the vowels you see in translated Egyptian texts are only approximations of sounds which are used by Western Egyptologists to help them pronounce the Ancient Egyptian terms/words.

3. We will be using the most commonly-recognized words for the English-speaking people that identify a neter/netert [god, goddess], a pharaoh, or a city; followed by other 'variations' of such a word/term.

It should be noted that the real names of the deities (gods, goddesses) were kept secret so as to guard the cosmic power of the deity. The Neteru were referred to by epithets that describe particular quality, attribute, and/or aspect(s) of their roles. Such applies to all common terms such as Isis, Osiris, Amun, Re, Horus, etc.

4. When using the Latin calendar, we will use the following terms:

BCE – Before Common Era. Also noted in other references as BC.

CE – Common Era. Also noted in other references as AD.

5. The term Baladi will be used throughout this book to denote the present silent majority of Egyptians that adhere to the Ancient Egyptian traditions, with a thin exterior layer of Islam.[Read *Ancient Egyptian Culture Revealed* by Moustafa Gadalla for detailed information.]

REGIONAL MAP OF EGYPT

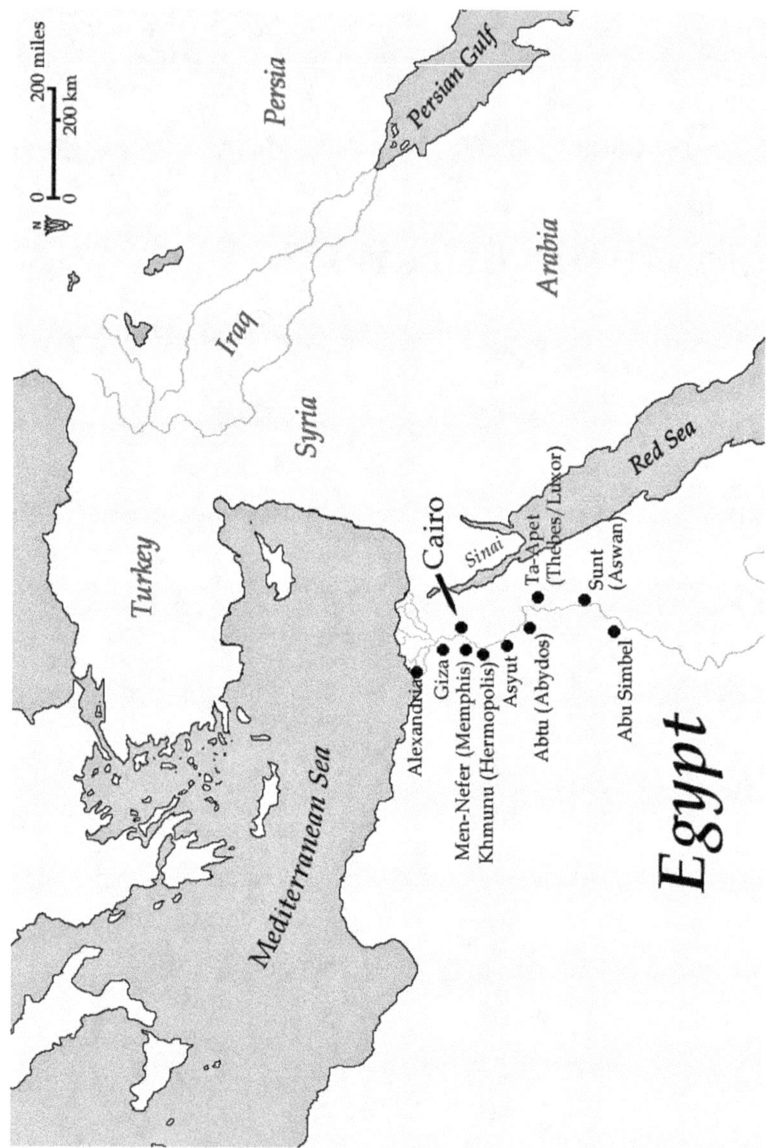

200 miles
200 km
N
Persia
Persian Gulf
Iraq
Arabia
Syria
Red Sea
Turkey
Cairo
Sinai
Ta-Apet (Thebes/Luxor)
Sunt (Aswan)
Alexandria
Giza
Men-Nefer (Memphis)
Khmunu (Hermopolis)
Asyut
Abtu (Abydos)
Abu Simbel
Mediterranean Sea
Egypt

Prelude: 'Imagine' by John Lennon

In 1971, John Lennon released his song 'Imagine', which appears to describe wishful thinking of an *ideal utopia*. The 'dreamy' lyrics, unbeknowst to its author, described the conditions of the longest civilization in the history of the world. The following chapters will show that John Lennon was describing the real lasting civilization of Ancient Egypt. Here are the lyrics of 'Imagine':

Imagine there's no heaven
It's easy if you try
No hell below us
Above us only sky
Imagine all the people
Living for today…

Imagine there're no countries
It isn't hard to do
Nothing to kill or die for
And no religion too
Imagine all the people
Living life in peace…

You may say I'm a dreamer
But I'm not the only one
I hope someday you'll join us
And the world will be as one

Imagine no possessions
I wonder if you can
No need for greed or hunger
A brotherhood of man
Imagine all the people
Sharing all the world…

You may say I'm a dreamer
But I'm not the only one
I hope someday you'll join us
And the world will live as one

Rediscover Egypt Anew

Despite the bad image of Ancient Egypt that has been embedded in our minds, there are two primary certain, acknowledged facts that should get our attention to rediscover Egypt anew:

1. The duration of the Egyptian civilization is the longest in the history of the whole world.

2. Herodotus, the Father of history, wrote in 500 BCE:

> *"Of all the nations of the world the Egyptians are the happiest, healthiest and most religious."*

These two simple facts should make us wonder how and why did that happen? One should wonder if some or several aspects of this long-lasting civilization can help us in our present times.

Can Egypt be the Ancient Future of the world? Can the conditions in Ancient Egypt be the archetypal ideal society that John Lennon recited in his song 'Imagine'? The bold answer is a resounding yes, as will be unfolded throughout this short book.

3

The Heavenly Angels of Egypt

3.1 THE HEAVENLY ANGELS OF EGYPT

It is commonly and wrongly popularized that Egyptians had a confused religious system with an indefinite number of gods and goddesses!

In reality the so-called "gods and goddesses" of Egypt and their functions were adopted and renamed "Angles" in the Bible. The Song of Moses in Deuteronomy (32:43), as found in a cave at Qumran near the Dead Sea, mentions the word *gods* in the plural:

> *"Rejoice, O heavens, with him; and do obeisance to him, ye gods".*

When the passage is quoted in the New Testament (Hebrews, 1:6), the word gods is substituted with

> *"angels of God".*

3.2 MONOTHEISM & POLYTHEISM

When we ask "Who is God?", we are really asking "What is God?". The mere name or noun does not tell us anything. One can only define "God" through the multitude of "His" attributes/qualities/powers/actions. To know "God" is to know the numerous qualities of "God". The more we learn of these qualities (known as neteru), the closer we get to our divine origin.

Far from being a primitive, polytheistic form, this is the highest expression of monotheistic mysticism.

The Egyptians regarded the universe as a conscious act of creation by the One Great God. The fundamental doctrine was the unity of the Deity. This One God was never represented. It is the functions and attributes of his domain that were represented. Once a reference was made to his functions/attributes, he became a distinguishable agent, reflecting this particular function/attribute and its influence on the world. His various functions and attributes as the Creator, Healer, and the like, were called the neteru (singular; neter in the masculine form and netert in the feminine form). As such, an Egyptian neter/netert was not a *god/goddess* but the representation of a function/ attribute of the One God.

The neteru, who were called 'gods' by some, were endorsed and incorporated into Christianity under a new name, 'angels'.

3.3 NETERU—THE DIVINE ENERGIES

Egyptian texts indicate that when the Master of the Universe came into existence, the whole creation came into existence. The Ancient Egyptian texts emphasize that the *Complete One* contains all. The Ancient Egyptian text reads:

> *"I am many of names and many of forms, and my Being exists in every neter".*

The Divine energy that manifests itself in the creation cycle is defined by its constituent energy aspects, called neteru by the Ancient Egyptians. The NeTeRu are the forces of NaTuRe.

The Egyptian word neter or nature or netjer means *a power that is able to generate life and to maintain it when generated.* As all parts of creation go through the cycle of birth-life-death-rebirth, so do the driving energies, during the stages of this cycle.

It is therefore that the Ancient Egyptian neteru, being divine energies, went and continue to go through the same cycle of birth-growth-death and renewal. Such understanding was common to all, as noted by Plutarch: that the multitude forces of nature known as neteru are born or created, subject to continuous changes, age and die, and are reborn.

We can give the example of the caterpillar that is born, lives, then builds its own cocoon, where it dies (or better yet, transforms into a butterfly), who lays eggs, and on and on. What we have here is the cyclical transformation from one form/state of energy to another.

Another example is the water cycle—the water that evaporates, forming clouds that rain back to Earth. It is all an orderly cyclical transformation of energies in various forms—*the death of one state and the rebirth of another.*

When you think of neteru not as *"gods and goddesses"* but as cosmic energy forces, one can see the Ancient Egyptian system as a brilliant representation of the universe. Philosophically, this cyclical natural transformation is akin to our saying:

"The more things change, the more they stay the same".

In scientific circles, this is known as the *natural law of conservation of energy*, which is described as: **the principle that energy is never consumed, but only changes form, and that the total energy in a physical system, such as the universe, cannot be increased or diminished.**

3.4 A MATTER OF ENERGIES

The Ancient and Baladi Egyptians made/make no distinction between a metaphysical state of being and one with a material body. Such a distinction is a mental illusion. We exist on a number of different levels at once, from the most physical to the most metaphysical. Einstein agreed with the same principles.

Since Einstein's relativity theory, it has been known and accepted that matter is a form of energy—a coagulation or condensation of energy. Energy is made up of molecules rotating or vibrating at various rates of speed. In the "physical" world, molecules rotate at a very slow and constant rate of speed. That is why things appear to be solid, to our earthly senses. The slower the speed, the more dense or solid the thing. In the metaphysical (spirit) world, the molecules vibrate in a much faster, or ethereal, dimension where things are freer and less dense.

In this light, the universe is basically a hierarchy of energies at different orders of density. Our senses have some access to the densest form of energy, which is matter. The hierarchy of energies is interrelated, and each level is sustained by the level below it. This hierarchy of energies is set neatly into a vast matrix of deeply interfaced natural laws. It is both physical and metaphysical.

This matrix of energies came as a result of the initial act of creation. This matrix of energies was identified with the neteru (gods/goddesses) in Ancient Egypt.

The presence of energy in everything was long recognized by the Ancient and Baladi Egyptians. That there are cosmic energies (neteru) in every stone, mineral, wood, etc., is stated clearly in the Shabaka Stele (8th century BCE):

> **And so the neteru** (gods, goddesses)**entered into their bodies, in the form of every sort of wood, of every sort of mineral, as every sort of clay, as everything which grows upon him** (meaning earth).

The universal energy matrix encompasses the world as a product of a complex system of relationships among people (living and dead), animals, plants, and natural and supernatural phenomena. This rationale is often called **Animism** because of its central premise that all things are animated (energized) by life forces. Each minute particle of everything is in constant motion, i.e. energized, as acknowledged in kinetic theory. In other words, everything is animated (energized)—animals, trees, rocks, birds—even the air, sun, and moon.

The faster form of energies—these invisible energies in the universe—are called 'spirits', by many. Spirits/energies are organized at different orders of densities, which relates to the different speeds of molecules. These faster (invisible) energies inhabit certain areas, or are associated with particular natural phenomena. Spirits (energies) exist in family-type groups (they are related to each other).

Energies may occupy, at will, a more condensed energy (matter) such as human, animal, plant, or any form. The spirit animates the human body at birth and leaves it at death. Sometimes more than one energy spirit enters a body. We often hear that a person is 'not feeling himself/herself', or is 'temporarily insane', 'possessed', 'beside oneself', or who has multiple personalities. The energies (spirits) have an effect on all of us, to one degree or another.

Since the created universe is orderly, its energy matrix is likewise a well-oiled machine with nine interpenetrating and interacting realms.

3.5 OUT OF EGYPT

The very thing that is now called the Christian religion was already in existence in Ancient Egypt long before the adoption of the New Testament. The British Egyptologist Sir E. A. Wallis Budge wrote in his book, *The Gods of the Egyptians* [1969]:

> *"The new religion (Christianity) which was preached there*

by St. Mark and his immediate followers, in all essentials so closely resembled that which was the outcome of the worship of Osiris, Isis, and Horus".

The similarities noted by Budge and everyone who has compared the Egyptian Osiris/Isis/Horus allegory to the Gospel story are striking. Both accounts are practically the same: the supernatural conception, the divine birth, the struggles against the enemy in the wilderness, and the resurrection from death to eternal life. The main difference between the "two versions" is that the Gospel tale is considered historical and the Osiris/Isis/Horus cycle is an allegory. The spiritual message of the Ancient Egyptian Osiris/Isis/Horus allegory and the Christian revelation is exactly the same.

The British scholar A.N. Wilson pointed out in his book, *Jesus*:

"The Jesus of History and the Christ of Faith are two separate beings, with very different stories. It is difficult enough to reconstruct the first, and in the attempt we are likely to do irreparable harm to the second".

There is an undeniable irony and a profound, deep, undeniable truth in Hosea's prophetic saying, *"Out of Egypt have I called my Son."* A deep irony, indeed.

3.6 EGYPTIAN COSMOLOGY AND ALLEGORIES

The cosmological knowledge of Ancient Egypt was expressed in story form, which is a superior means for expressing both physical and metaphysical concepts. Well-crafted allegories are the only way to explain the deepest truths about God, creation, life, the soul, our place in the universe, and our struggle to evolve to higher levels of insight and understanding.

Allegories are an intentionally chosen means for communicating knowledge. Allegories dramatize cosmic laws, principles, processes, and relationships and functions, and express them in an easy-to-understand way. Once the inner meanings of the allegories have been revealed, they become marvels of simultaneous scientific and philosophical completeness and conciseness. The more they are studied, the richer they become. The 'inner dimension' of the teachings embedded into each story are capable of revealing several layers of knowledge, according to the stage of development of the listener. The "secrets" are revealed as one evolves higher. The higher we get, the more we see. It is always there.

Any good writer or lecturer knows that stories are the best means for explaining the behavior of things, because the relationships of parts to each other, and to the whole, are better maintained by the mind. The Egyptian sages transformed common factual nouns and adjectives (indicators of qualities) into proper but conceptual nouns. These were, in addition, personified so that they could be woven into narratives.

The Egyptians did not believe their allegories to be *historical facts*. They believed IN them, in the sense that they believed in the truth behind the stories.

The Ancient Egyptians had numerous allegories, such as the Osiris/Isis/Horus allegory.

4

Discover The Powers Within You

4.1 TAKING CONTROL OF YOUR PERSONAL LIFE

While others insist that all humans were *"born sinners"*, the Egyptian teachings emphasize and build on the positive idea that within each human being is a "treasure" which can be found only by looking for it. The Egyptian teachings unleash the inner hidden potential of the human being to recognize and balance the energies within to learn, gain knowledge, and achieve.

Each one of us must know how to manage these energies within and around ourselves, including all the forces, desires, emotions, etc. within each of us. Social laws must follow the same pattern of the energy organization of the universe. As Above So Below.

In concentrations, especially when they are massive and uncontrolled, this energy matrix within is potentially dangerous; even deadly. Being hyperactive or angry are human examples of uncontrolled massive energies. It is therefore of paramount importance that the energy matrix be understood, managed, and controlled.

The principle of cosmic order on all levels, including human beings, is simply called 'Maat' by the Egyptians. Ma-at is the netert (goddess) that represents the principle of cosmic order; the concept by which not only men, but also the neteru (gods, goddesses) themselves were governed; and without which the neteru (gods, goddesses) are functionless.

To solve any problem in your life, you need to empower your Maat within to bring order, balance, and harmony. Maat will guide you in sorting out (giving definition to/bringing order to) all the chaos (the undifferentiated energy/matter and consciousness) within. More about Maat later on in this chapter.

4.2 PURSUE YOUR OWN PATH TO THE SOURCE

In Egypt, what we now call *'religion'* was so widely acknowledged that it did not even need a name, because it is life itself in all its aspects. All the knowledge that was based on cosmic consciousness was embedded into their daily practices, which became traditions.

The Egyptian model is not about the outer world or a community of believers, dogma, scriptures, rules, or rituals. It is not about simply believing that God is this or God is that or that. It is not just asking one to "believe", and one is automatically in God's graces. The Egyptian model of consists of ideas and practices that provide the tools for any spiritual seeker to progress along each one's Path towards "union with the Divine".

This spiritual Path towards union requires one to engage in the hard and sometimes painful (but joyful) commitment to inner and outer purification. The seeker must gain knowledge of reality/truth, do well in everything, and apply what he/she has learned in the world. It is a philosophy of life; a way of individual behavior in order to achieve the highest morality and internal happiness and peace.

The general perception of mysticism is that it is possible to achieve communion with God by attaining knowledge of spiritual truth through intuition acquired by fixed meditation. The

Egyptian model for gaining knowledge is based on the utilization of both intellect and intuition.

The natural principles and practices of the Egyptian model are as common in the West as in the East. A mystical seeker is anyone who believes that it is possible to have a direct experience of God. The Egyptian model of mysticism is a natural expression of personal religion. The seeker has the right to pursue a life of contemplation, seeking contact with the Source of being and reality. The mystical seekers pursue knowledge of the Reality/Truth of God that cannot be gained through dogmatic religions.

The Egyptian model of mysticism (Sufism) is not a matter of creed and dogma, but rather a personal charter. Each one of us is a unique individual. The Ancient Egyptians implemented their beliefs in the individuality of each of us, in all their texts. For example, there were never two identical transformational (funerary) or medical (so-called "magical") texts for any two individuals. There is no one-size-fits-all dogmatic doctrine.

The Egyptian model recognizes the uniqueness of each individual, and as such, recognizes that the Paths to God are as numerous as the number of seekers. The ways to God are like the streams—they all go to one source. All Egyptian thinking is based on this principle of *variation on a theme.*

The mystical seekers generate their own kinds of collective life. Like-minded seekers form networks of masters and disciples called the *Ways*. The framework of a *Way* is better described as a *fellowship*. An Egyptian model mystic fellowship (order) can be formed anytime and anywhere.

The diversity of humankind is reflected in the diversity of fellowships. Hence, fellowships vary in their nature, teachings, exercises, etc.

The progression along the spiritual Path is acquired through striving, and is a matter of conscious disciplined action. Each new/raised consciousness is equivalent to a new awakening. The levels of consciousness are referred to as death—rebirth. Such thinking has pervaded Ancient (and present-day) Egypt, where birth and rebirth are a constant theme. The word *death* is employed in a figurative sense. The theme that man must *"die before he dies"* or that he must be *"born again"* in his present life is taken symbolically, or is commemorated by a ritual. In this, the candidate has to pass through certain specific experiences (technically termed "deaths"). A good example is baptism, which was the main objective at Easter, after Lent, representing the *death* of the old self by immersion into water, and rising the new/renewed self by resurfacing out of the water.

4.3 THE MORES AND MORALS OF MAAT

According to Egyptian philosophy, although all creation is spiritual in origin, man is born mortal but contains within himself the seed of the divine. His purpose in this life is to nourish that seed, and his reward, if successful, is eternal life, where he will reunite with his divine origin. Nourishing plants in the soil is analogous to nourishing the spirit on Earth by doing good deeds.

Man comes into the world with higher divine faculties, which are the essence of his/her salvation, in an unawakened state. The way of the Egyptian religion is, therefore, a system of practices aimed at awakening these dormant higher faculties.

The faculty-awakening emphasis of Egyptian religion cannot be over stressed. Moral behavior, for example, does not come about from merely learning certain values, but is gained by the mind and acquired by experience. Inner purification must be completed by practicing good social behavior daily in life. Every action impresses itself upon the heart. The inward being of a person is really the reflection of his deeds and actions. Doing good deeds thus establishes good inner qualities; the virtues impressed upon the heart in turn govern the actions of the limbs. As each act, thought, and deed makes an image on the heart, it becomes an attribute of the person. This maturation of the soul through acquired attributes leads to progressive mystical visions and the ultimate unification with the Divine.

Ancient Egyptian wisdom has always laid great emphasis on the cultivation of ethical behavior and service to society. The Egyptian traditions and practices emphasize character building, good behavior, family values, desirability, and the benefits of marriage, harmonic relationships, societal duties, work ethics, accountability, etc.

One must live his/her own life, and each one of us must go his/her own way, guided by Ma-at. The concept of Ma-at has permeated all Egyptian writings, from the earliest times and throughout Egyptian history. Ma-at is not easily translated or defined by one word. Basically, we might say that it means that which, of right, should be; that which is according to the proper order and harmony of the cosmos and of neteru and men, who are part of it.

Ma-at, *The Way*, encompasses the virtues, goals, and duties that define acceptable, if not ideal, social interactions and personal behavior.

A summary of the Egyptian concept of righteousness can be found in what is popularly known as the *Negative Confessions*. A more detailed picture of a righteous man and the expected conduct and the ideas of responsibility and retribution can be obtained from the walls of tomb chapels and in several literary compositions that are usually termed as 'wisdom texts' of systematic instructions, composed of maxims and precepts. Among them are the 30 chapters of the *Teaching of Amenemope (Amenhotep III)*, which contain many wisdom texts that were later adopted in the *Old Testament's Book of Proverbs*.

5

Making Democracy Work!

5.1 PRESENT PROBLEMS AND OLD SOLUTIONS

In all democratic countries citizens are dissatisfied with their governance system and claim that it does not represent their interests. Many defend the status quo by saying that the alternative is worse.

Here are some recognizable major problems:

- Money influence in politics
- Special interests lobbyists in decision-making processes of the governance system
- Career politicians and not community representatives
- A total paralysis between branches of government–individual voting on candidates is based on a personality contest and not true representation, like 'which candidate would you have a beer with?!' or 'Which candidate looks stiffer than the other!'
- Political parties' distinctions are so muted that in many cases there is no real practical difference and the results will favor those with more money and/or more 'magnetic personality'!

But there are alternatives to fix present problems by going to the untainted origin of such a system. It has been said and repeated that Greece is the source of democracy and the democratic system of governance. Shear repetitions of things may make people feel good, but on merits, repetition will not make them *facts* without supporting evidence!

Let us revisit the untainted Egyptian source which Plato adopted in his writings of the Republic, Laws and others parts of his collected writings.

5.2 COMMONWEALTH VS. CENTRALIZED GOVERNMENT

It's commonly accepted by all politicians at all levels of government that **'All Politics are local'**. The Ancient Egyptian system, being a truly grassroots system, starts at the local level. In order to protect the individuality of the polity and its sociopolitical coherence, a co-op system between several polities was needed. This would be the commonwealth-type alliance, where coalitions are formed to share specific duties and responsibilities that can benefit all of them. This was organized—as confirmed by Strabo—into basically three levels: local community, district jurisdiction(county), and province (state). These organizational forms varied from one area to another, and from one era to another. Ancient Egyptians had traditions of these non-coercive political organizations.

Unlike the autocratic, centralized type of government, the form of a commonwealth-type government recognizes the importance of grassroots *local communities.*

Coalitions are formed to share specific duties and responsibilities that can benefit everyone, such as communal public projects, trades, treaties of non-aggression, rights of passage, etc.

Contrary to academia's autocratic thinking, the Ancient Egyptian organizational government was not formed from the top (pharaoh) to the bottom (local community). It was formed from the bottom to the top—from local communities to districts to regional and "national"—each under its selected governance.

Each organizational level was the same form, only mirrored on a smaller/larger scale, being a representative council with its administrative superintendents.

The elders, representing the established lineages of the community, formed a council (legislative body) which elected a headman. This eldership assisted the headman in the governance of the community. The council of elders served as a court that helped the headman allocate access to resources (such as land, water rights, etc.), organize public works, etc.

The Ancient Egyptian political system was consistent with our present-time slogans of *"limited government", "government by necessity", "the best government is the least government"*, and *"government from the people, by the people, and for the people".*

Alliances between communities/regions can be resolved, changed, or restructured—i.e. *government by necessity*—for specific purpose(s) and/or duration(s), and they did so throughout Ancient Egyptian history. We should not misunderstand such changes to mean upheaval/chaos, but the true application of *Live and Let Live.* This is a true grassroots democracy. An example would be the state of the whole land of Egypt during this 22nd Dynasty, which may be deduced from the long inscription of King Takelot II (860-835 BCE) in the temple of Karnak. From this text, it is clear that there were several regional governments, each with their own king/leader. There were no signs of wars or strife during this time, contrary to Western academia's perception.

Western academia is obsessed with a centralized type of government, believing that the lack of such a governance type means chaos, strife, and civil war, etc!

The Egyptian system is the true form of a grassroots republic democracy that was the source of Plato's *Collected Dialogues* on the subjects of Laws and Republic.

5.3 PEOPLE PARTICIPATION

Individuals have the right to choose their local representatives who will represent the collective interests of a community on all levels. To choose a representative for a special purpose/mission/task, a caucus was conducted.

In matters of regular local nature, an individual may participate in their local council/elders public meetings. Also, an individual may submit a petition on any matter and a response was mandatory from the authorities in charge, as evident in hundreds of recovered Ancient Egyptian papyri.

5.4 FAIR TAXATION WITH JUSTIFICATION

There was no income tax of any kind. There were user's fees for gaining a particular access and/or service. It was a truly free market system with minimal governmental interference. It was a vibrant market economy.

A community council may impose a justifiable proportioned fee for a specific duration to raise funds for a particular project. Only affected/benefited parties were obliged to pay. In short, there were specific-purpose taxes/fees and never a *general* taxation which went to the treasury for spending on "general" purposes!

5.5 ROOTS AND REMEDIES OF INTERNAL CONFLICTS

In a society, the paramount feature should be *'one for all and all for one'*. Having grassroots democratic representation ensures peaceful existence between all. Conflicts, if any, were resolved in several ways, depending on the complexity of the issue. For more detailed information, read *Ancient Egyptian Culture Revealed* by Moustafa Gadalla.

5.6 EXTERNAL CONFLICTS—WAR AND PEACE

As will be explained in a later chapter, there was no such thing as *ownership* of land. One had the right to lease a piece of land for one reason or another, and paid a leasing fee. The sociopolitical system described above, of *'live and let live',* does not create this false sense of *"nationalism"* governed by artificial borders. As such, boundary conflicts were minimal.

It is widely recognized that the Egyptians (ancient and present) are an un-warlike people. It is therefore that Egypt was not interested in an empire, and certainly not in military occupation. Egypt was only interested in neutralizing the hostile elements that threatened to disrupt her own security. Egypt had to rely almost exclusively on foreign mercenaries for such a task. The pharaohs of the New Kingdom utilized diplomacy and marriage to foreign princesses to avoid conflict, with force only being used when all else failed.

War, for the Ancient Egyptians, followed rules as strict as a chess game, and had specific rituals. They were truly the civilized people. A war had a profound religious significance. It symbolized the forces of order controlling chaos and the light triumphing over darkness.

In Ancient Egyptian temples, tombs, and texts, human vices are depicted as foreigners (the sick body is sick because it is/was invaded by foreign germs). Foreigners are depicted as subdued—arms tightened/tied behind their backs—to portray inner self-control. The most vivid example of self control is the common depiction of the Pharaoh (The Perfected Man) on the outer walls of Ancient Egyptian temples, subduing/controlling *foreign enemies*—the *enemies (impurities) within.*

The same "war" scene is repeated at temples throughout the country, which signifies its symbolism and is not a representation of actual historical events. The "war" scenes symbolize the never-ending battle between Good and Evil.

Western academics are incapable of understanding metaphysical realities, and hence "make" historical events out of metaphysical concepts. The famed *"Battle of Kadesh"* is really the personal drama of the individual 'divine man' (the king in each of us) single-handedly **subduing the inner forces** of chaos and darkness. 'Kadesh' means holy/ sacred. Therefore, the Battle of Kadesh **signifies the inner struggle**—a holy war within each individual.

6

Dealing With Mother Earth

6.1 TENANTS NOT OWNERS

The concept of land, to the Egyptians (Ancient and Baladi), doesn't accept the premise that land is a property that can be owned. To them, people have the right to occupy a land only if they work it, and they can only own the fruit of their labor. The Ancient Egyptians had no verb meaning *'to possess'*, *'to have'*, nor any verb meaning *'to belong to'*.

Farmers are allowed access to the land only if they cultivate it. This concept of land is found in many countries in the world and is called 'public land' (or some other similar term). The idea is that the land is "owned" by the government (meaning, people) and access is provided for the people to work it in a certain way (mining, grazing, etc.).

The farmers' work was/is closely associated with local (and regional) water resource superintendents.

6.2 TREAD LIGHTLY

The Ancient and Baladi Egyptian beliefs in Animism were also reflected in their traditional relationships between people and earth. The Egyptians believed/believe that land had no value apart from people, and, conversely, that people could not exist without land. They recognize and respect the supernatural residents of the land—any land. The spirits of a place (trees, rock outcroppings, rivers, snakes, and other animals and objects) were identified and placated by the original founders who arrived and inhabited the land at an earlier time. The spirits of the land might vary with each place, or be so closely identified with a group's welfare that they were carried to a new place as part of the continuity of a group with its former home.

The rights of a group, defined by common genealogical descent, were linked to a particular place and the settlements within it not through "ownership", but because of their pact with the primordial spirits of the land/site. The spirits, both of family and place, demanded loyalty to communal virtues and to the authority of the elders in maintaining ancient beliefs and practices.

Newcomers (spiritual migrants) join the local spirit population in a new covenant between themselves and the local spirits. This covenant legitimized their arrival. In return for regular homage to these spirits, the founders could claim perpetual access to local resources. In so doing, they became the lineage in charge of the hereditary local priesthood and village headship, and were/are recognized by later human arrivals as "tenants of the place".

6.3 KEEP IT CLEAN

This spirit of Animism makes people environmentalists, for they treat everything with care and respect. Such coexistence with nature in all its forms was a mandatory requirement of each person. Here are a few of the well-known Ancient Egyptian 42 Negative Confessions that emphasize that one must be true environmentalist in order to succeed in reuniting with the Source:

7- I have not plundered the neteru.

16- I have not laid waste the ploughed land.

22- I have not polluted myself.

34- I have not fouled the water.

36- I have never cursed the neteru.

Neteru means the divine essence (spirits) living in everything—plants, air, water, minerals, etc.

6.4 PEACE ON EARTH

Such respect for the spirits of the land is indicative of a peaceful (non-invasive) people who will not violate anybody or any land. Egyptians, as such, are very peaceful people. For the Ancient and Baladi Egyptians, stepping on foreign land in peace or in war was done with careful consideration for the land and all its inhabitants, human or otherwise.

Discover The Masonic Powers of Egypt

7.1 THE EGYPTIAN MASONIC SYMPHONY

The masons claim that their rites, knowledge, and traditions are rooted in Egypt. The masons are members of a widespread secret fraternal society called *'Free and Accepted Masons'* (popularly known as Freemasonry). There is a natural, instinctive fellowship and sympathy between their members.

Modern masons claim their deep roots from the Ancient Egyptians. It is interesting that the obelisk and the pyramid were important symbolic forms for them long before Egyptology and archaeology began. The Founding Fathers of America (many of whom were masons) put the un-American pyramid on the dollar bill and chose the shape of an obelisk for the design of a monument for George Washington, who was also a mason.

Herodotus, the father of history and a native Greek, stated, in 500 BCE:

> *"Now, let me talk more of Egypt for it has a lot of admirable things and what one sees there is superior to any other country."*

The superior Ancient Egyptian monuments are the physical manifestations of their superior cosmic knowledge, for, as stated in Asleptus III (25) of Hermetic Texts:

Therefore, we must forego viewing the Ancient Egyptian monuments as interplays of forms against a vague historical, archaeological presentation. Instead, we must try to see it as the dwelling place of the cosmos; as the relationship between form and function.

Johann Wolfgang Von Goethe (1749-1832) described architecture as "frozen music". In Ancient Egypt, architecture was animated visual music—definitely not frozen. Egyptian architecture and art followed the principles of harmonic dynamic design that equally applies to sound and form.

Sound and form are two sides of the same coin, and their relationship is equated to the metaphysical and physical aspects of the universe.

The physical manifestation of the universe is a masterpiece of order, harmony, and beauty. The architecture of bodily existence is determined by an invisible, immaterial world of pure form and geometry.

The Ancient Egyptians, who were/are known as doers (builders), put their knowledge and wisdom into animated, energetic, productive works.

The design of Ancient Egyptian architecture was based on harmonic proportion. Musical harmonies are likewise based on harmonic proportion. It has been said that music is, in reality, geometry translated into sound; for in music the same harmonies can be heard that underlie architectural proportion.

The famed Mozart was a Mason, just like his father and many

notable people in his era. His music was the spirit of past Ancient Egyptian traditions. His crowning achievement was the Masonic Opera, where the power of masonry becomes the power of music by using *Masonic symbols.*

7.2 PERSONAL MONUMENTS OR ENERGY GENERATORS

It is a common tendency to ignore the religious function of the Ancient Egyptian temples. We must try to see this as the relationship between form and function. Instead, they are viewed by many as merely an art gallery and/or an interplay of forms against a vague historical presentation.

In reality, the Egyptian temple was the link and the proportional mean between the macrocosmos (world) and microcosmos (man). It was a stage upon which meetings were enacted between the neteru (gods/goddesses) and the king, as a representative of the people.

The Egyptian temple was a machine for generating and maintaining divine energy for the benefit of one and all. It was the place in which the cosmic energy of the neteru (gods/goddesses) came to dwell and radiate their energies to the land and people.

The harmonious power of the temple plans, the images engraved on the walls, and the forms of worship all led to the same goal; a goal that was spiritual (as it involved setting superhuman forces in motion) and practical (in that the final awaited result was the maintenance of the country's prosperity).

The choice of location and design peculiarities of a temple were not based on economical considerations, but rather on a deeper knowledge of the macro cosmos.

The Egyptian temples were not built quickly, or by one king alone. Such temples were built over the centuries, by successive kings. A good example is the huge complex of the great Karnak Temples, which was built over a span of more than 1,500 years. The Karnak Temples features six pylons, and is an imposing and homogeneous achievement that produced a harmonious plan of buildings covering about 7,550 ft. [2,300 m] in perimeter. It is obvious that the overall plan pre-existed and that it was known to those who made the additions over a span of more than 1,500 years.

7.3 ARCHITECTURE AND SACRED GEOMETRY

Harmonic design in Ancient Egyptian architecture was achieved through a unification of two systems:

1. arithmetic (significant numbers along a center-line axis)

2. graphic (square, rectangles, and a few triangles)

The union of the two systems reflects the relationship of the parts to the whole, which is the essence of harmonic design.

Significant points were determined along the design axis. These points mark the intersection with transverse axes, the alignment of a central doorway, the position of an altar, the center of a sanctuary, etc. These significant points follow a precise arithmetic progression. In many of the best plans, these significant points are at harmonic distances from one another, and their distances from one end to the other express the figures of the Summation (so-called Fibonacci) Series, 2, 3, 5, 8, 13, 21, 34, 55, 89, 144, 233, 377, 610, . . . The harmonic analysis shows a series of significant points readable from both ends; i.e., if inverted, a system of significant points would also correspond to the Series, with the reference point starting at the opposite end of the plan.

The Summation Series was utilized in the Egyptian monuments ever since the Old Kingdom. The design of the pyramid temple of Khafra (Chephren) at Giza reaches the figure of 233 cubits in its total length, as measured from the pyramid, with a complete series of TEN significant points. The Karnak Temple follows the Summation Series' figures up to 610 cubits – i.e. TWELVE significant points. [See diagrams of several Ancient Egyptian temples in *Ancient Egyptian Metaphysical Architecture* by Moustafa Gadalla.]

7.4 LET ENERGY FLOW

In order to maintain the unity of the temple, its components must be connected so that the cosmic energy can flow throughout its parts unimpeded.

The unity of the components of the temple must be like the components of the human body. The walls of a temple consist of blocks and corners, and such components (blocks) must be connected together in a way that allows the flow of divine energy, just like the parts of the human being. It is incorrect to merely think that a connection between two components/parts is only to ensure the structural stability of the part(s) and the whole building.

We can take clues from the human body (the house of the soul) when reviewing the Egyptian temple (the house of cosmic soul/ energy/neteru). The human body is connected with muscles, etc., but veins and nerves are not interrupted at the bone joints of the skeleton. The living Ancient Egyptian temple was designed likewise. Basreliefs of all sizes, as well as the hieroglyphic symbols, span two adjoining blocks with total perfection. The intent is very clear: to bridge over the joint between adjacent blocks (next to each other, or on top of each other).

The blocks themselves were joined together in some type of nerve/energy system. A continuation of energy flow required special interlocking patterns. The practice of joining blocks together prevailed in every Egyptian temple throughout the known history of Ancient Egypt. [See more detailed information in *Ancient Egyptian Metaphysical Architecture* by Moustafa Gadalla.]

7.5 PYRAMID POWER

We were taught in schools that the pyramids are nothing but tombs which were built by tyrant Pharaohs, and that slaves were used to haul these big stones up temporary ramps in the construction of these pyramids. These commonly held views are without any evidence.

When one examines the facts, especially as one visits the pyramids, one will find that commonly held beliefs about the pyramids are so incredibly illogical that you may doubt yourself.

Here we provide a little information about 'Pyramid power'. Many researchers found that there was some property in the pyramidal shape that made it responsible for extraordinary powers. They experimented with various items by placing each item in the equivalent position of the "King's Room" within a scaled model of a correctly oriented pyramid. They found out that highly perishable materials were preserved, blunt, old-fashioned carbon steel razor blades regained their sharp edges after an overnight stay, etc. Many concluded that the pyramidal shape itself was responsible, and somehow changed the physical, chemical, and biological processes that might take place within that shape. This experimentation led to the phenomenon known as "Pyramid Power".

One feels the power of these Egyptian pyramids when inside or outside them because their configurations are harmonically proportioned.

The pyramids were harmonically proportioned to act/function in the same fashion as *greenhouses* – i.e. to attract and retain certain energies. In the case of the Egyptian pyramid, it should be called the *bluehouse* effect.

In the case of greenhouse effect, it is the retention of heat from sunlight at the earth's surface, caused by atmospheric carbon dioxide, that admits shortwave radiation but absorbs the long wave radiation emitted by the Earth.

In the case of the *bluehouse* effect, the building retains the orgone energy. Orgone comes from outer space. It is what makes the stars twinkle, and the sky blue.

The subject of the pyramids cannot be covered in a few pages. For a comprehensive coverage of this subject, read *Egyptian Pyramids Revisited* by Moustafa Gadalla.

The Writings on The [Egyptian] Wall

8.1 THE CHARACTER OF EGYPTIAN ART

Art, like anything in Egyptian life, was a part of the Master Plan of man and the universe. The Egyptians were able to reduce their universal environment into a rational and finite system. Accordingly, art had a canon of proportion, to which it should conform. As a result, the ground plan and elevations of an Egyptian building, as well as statues, etc., reflected a particular and a meaningful mathematical order.

The careful definition of the separate planes of this cubical universe is revealed in an art which is essentially two-dimensional. In order to represent three-dimensional objects on a plane surface, the Egyptians avoided the perspectival solution of the problem. That resulted in a two-dimensional profile, with the exception of a few parts of the body, like the eyes and sometimes the horns.

The Egyptian artist presented, in his work, the idea of objects, rather than their exact realization in a spatial context. Their creative artistic concept is similar to God's creative actions. As a result of God's Word (utterance), the world was created.

Similarly, every creative work of art, even a statue, has inscriptions describing the action or defining its purpose as well as the names of the actors.

Additionally, each statue, painting, relief, or building had to undergo, upon its completion, the ritual of the *Opening of the Mouth* to ensure that it was transformed from an inanimate product of man's hands into a vibrant part of the divine order charged with numinous power.

The end result is an unfrozen, vibrant, dynamic, expressive, and active "art".

8.2 THE DYNAMIC WALLS (BAS-RELIEF)

The Egyptian sculptures, friezes, and paintings were carefully planned according to harmonic, geometric, and proportional laws.

The walls of the Egyptian temple were covered with animated images—including hieroglyphs—to facilitate the communication between the above and the below. The Ancient Egyptian framework was usually a square, representing the manifested world (squaring of the circle).

Additionally, the square grid itself had the symbolic meaning of the manifested world, which also made it easy to construct the root rectangles of 2, 3, and 5, from/within a square background. The corners of squares and root rectangles were defined by notches along the perimeter, or carefully defined by incised lines.

Design that is based on root rectangles is called **generative dynamic design**, which only the Egyptians practiced. Egyptian sacred objects and buildings have geometries based upon the division of space attained by the root rectangles and their derivatives, such as the Neb (Golden) Proportion.

The Egyptian bas-relief composition shows that its designer proportioned the picture, as well as the groups of hieroglyphs, by the application of whirling square rectangles to a square. The outlines of the major square are carefully incised into the stone by short bars.

Practically all figures on the walls of the Egyptian buildings are in profile form, indicative of action and interaction between the various symbolic figures. A wide variety of actions in the forms are evident. Wall depictions show very active and interactive actions with amazing symbolism.

A common example is how some figures are shown with two right/left hands. An active right hand symbolizes giving. An active left hand signifies receiving. When the symbolic role of the person is wholly active, he is shown with two right hands. When his role is wholly passive, he has two left hands.

8.3 COSMIC CONSCIOUSNESS OR MUNDANE ART

The scenes of daily activities, found inside Egyptian tombs, show a strong perpetual correlation between the Earth and heavens. The scenes provide graphical representations of all sorts of activities: hunting, fishing, agriculture, legal courts, and all kinds of arts and crafts. Portraying these daily activities in the presence of the neteru (gods, goddesses) or with their assistance signifies their cosmic correspondence—a strong perpetual correlation between the Earth and heavens.

This perpetual correlation—cosmic consciousness—was echoed in Asleptus III [25] of the Hermetic Texts:

> *"..in Egypt all the operations of the powers which rule and work in heaven have been transferred to earth below...it should rather be said that the whole cosmos dwells in [Egypt] as in its sanctuary..."*

Every action, no matter how mundane, had in some sense a cosmic corresponding act: plowing, sowing, reaping, brewing, the sizing of a beer mug, building ships, waging wars, playing games—all were viewed as earthly symbols for divine activities. In other words, **for Ancient (and Baladi) Egyptians, every 'physical' aspect of life had a symbolic (metaphysical) meaning. But also, every symbolic act of expression had a 'material' background. As Above So Below and As Below So Above.**

8.4 SYMBOLISM

A symbol, by definition, is not what it represents, but what it stands for; what it suggests. A symbol reveals to the mind a reality other than itself. Words convey information; symbols evoke understanding.

In the Egyptian temples, the Ancient Egyptians utilized pictorial symbols to represent metaphysical concepts. As the saying goes: *'a picture is worth a thousand words'*. In Egyptian symbolism, the precise role of the neteru (gods/goddesses) are revealed in many ways: by dress, headdress, crown, feathers, animal, plant, color, position, size, gesture, sacred object (e.g., flail, scepter, staff, ankh), etc. A chosen symbol represents that function or principle on all levels simultaneously—from the simplest, most obvious physical manifestation of that function to the most abstract and metaphysical. This symbolic language represents a wealth of physical, physiological, psychological and spiritual data in the presented symbols.

8.5 ANIMAL SYMBOLISM

To the Ancient Egyptians, each animal/bird symbolizes and embodies certain divine functions and principles in a particularly pure and striking fashion. As such, the animal or animal-headed neteru (gods/goddesses) are symbolic expressions of a deep spiritual understanding.

When a total animal is depicted in Ancient Egypt, it represents a particular function/attribute in its purest form. When an animal-headed figure is depicted, it conveys that particular function/attribute in the human being.

Let us take the example of the dog, which embodies the essence of spiritual guidance. The dog/jackal is known for its reliable homing instinct, day or night. The dog is very useful in searches, and is the animal of choice to guide the blind. As such, it is an excellent choice for guiding the soul of the deceased through the regions of the Duat.

The metaphysical role of Anubis, the dog, is reflected in his diet. The dog/jackal feasts on carrion, turning it into beneficial nourishment. In other words, Anubis represents the capacity to turn waste into useful food for the body (and soul)—as in the alchemical way of transforming lead into gold.

Several examples of animal symbolism can be found in *Egyptian Divinities: the All Who Are THE ONE,* by Moustafa Gadalla.

8.6 THE THREE ROLES OF EACH HIEROGLYPHIC IMAGE

The Ancient Egyptians' pictorial system is commonly called 'hieroglyphs', comprised of a large number of pictorial symbols. The word hieroglyph means 'holy script' (hieros = holy, glyphein = impress).

The metaphorical and symbolic concept of hieroglyphs was unanimously acknowledged by ALL early writers on the subject, such as Plutarch, Diodorus, Clement, etc.

The 'Hieroglyphics' of Horapollo' is the only true hieroglyphic treatise preserved from classical antiquity. It consists of two books; one containing 70 chapters, the other 119; each dealing with one particular hieroglyph. The relations between sign and meaning were, according to Horapollo, always of an allegorical nature, and it was always established by means of 'philosophical' reasoning. Accordingly, each hieroglyph has a short heading describing either the hieroglyph itself (in simple terms, as, for instance, 'the explanation of the picture of a falcon'), or else stating the nature of the allegorical subject to be explained, such as 'how to signify eternity' or 'how to signify the universe'.

Likewise, Clement of Alexandria, in *Stromata, Book V*, Chapter IV, tells us the two main roles (Literal and Symbolic) of the Egyptian hieroglyphs and how the later (Symbolic) contains two roles—figurative and allegoric [mystical]:

> *"The Egyptian Hieroglyphic, of which one aspect is by the first elements is literal, and the other Symbolic. Of the Symbolic, one kind speaks literally by imitation, and another writes as it were figuratively; and another is quite allegorical, using certain enigmas."*

[I] On the first role/subject—*literally, by imitation,* Clement, in *Stromata Book V*, Chapter IV, continues:

> *"Wishing to express Sun in writing, they make a circle; and Moon, a figure like the Moon, like its proper shape".*

[II] On the second role/subject—*figurative-* Clement in *Stromata, Book V*, Chapter IV, continues:

> *"But in using the figurative style, by transposing and transferring, by changing and by transforming in many ways as suits them, they draw characters".*

[III] On the third role/subject—*allegorical* – Clement, in *Stromata, Book V*, Chapter IV, continues:

> *"Let the following stand as a specimen of the third species-the Enigmatic. For the rest of the stars, on account of their oblique course, they have figured like the bodies of serpents; but the sun, like that of a beetle, because it makes a round figure of ox-*

dung, and rolls it before its face. And they say that this crea-
ture lives six months under ground, and the other division of
the year above ground, and emits its seed into the ball, and
brings forth; and that there is not a female beetle."

Clement, like ALL classical writers of antiquities, asserted that the Egyptian hieroglyphics represent true images of the divine law. The relations between sign and meaning were always of an allegorical nature, and it was always established by means of 'philosophical' reasoning.

To summarize: the symbolic Egyptian hieroglyphic writing is basically divided into three roles:

1) the Imitative (an object represents itself),

2) the Figurative (an object stands for one of its qualities) and

3) the Allegorical (an object is linked through enigmatic conceptual processes)

In fact, these categories describe relations between visual forms and their meanings. A visual form may be mimetic or imitative, directly copying features of the object it represents; it may be associative, suggesting attributes which are not visually present such as abstract properties incapable of literal depiction; and finally, it may be symbolic, meaningful only when decoded according to conventions or systems of knowledge which, though not inherently visual, are communicated through visual means.

Much more about this subject can be found in *The Egyptian Hiero-glyph Metaphysical Language* by Moustafa Gadalla.

Extent of The Ancient Egyptian Civilization

9.1 AGE OF THE ANCIENT EGYPTIAN CIVILIZATION

Herodotus reported that he was informed by Egyptian priests that *"the sun had twice set where it now rose, and twice risen where it now set."* The statement indicates that the Ancient Egyptians counted their history for more than one zodiac cycle of 25,920 years.

The Ancient Egyptian history extended to a complete zodiac cycle of 25,920 years, plus a partial zodiac cycle between 10948 BCE [the beginning point of our present zodiac cycle] and the end of the Age of Aries, when Ancient Egypt lost its independence. Thus, the antiquity of Ancient Egypt is [25,920 + (10,948 – 148)] 36,720 years old.

That the Ancient Egyptian civilization is over 36,000 years old—and, by extension, that life on Earth is that old—goes against Christian/Western establishments. As a result, it has been continuously repeated that the Pharaoh Mena (c. 31st century BCE) is reputed to have "unified Egypt" and began the Ancient Egyptian civilization.

The chronology of the Ancient Egyptian Pharaohs, since the time of Mena, came basically from Manetho in the 3rd century BCE. Manetho's work has not survived—we have only the commen-

taries on it by Sextus Africanus [c. 221 CE] and Eusebius of Cae-
sarea [c. 264–340 CE].

According to Eusebius, Manetho ascribed great antiquity to
Pharaonic Egypt with the age of the Ancient Egyptian antiquities
of 36,000 years, which is consistent with the accounts of
Herodotus. This is in general agreement with other accounts
and evidential findings, such as Diodorus of Sicily [Diodorus
I, 24] and the Ancient Egyptian document known as the Turin
Papyrus—an original Egyptian document dating from the 17th
Dynasty [c. 1400 BCE].

The physical evidence also supports this remote antiquity of
Ancient Egypt despite the fact that so much archaeological evidence from such remote times has been buried below present
groundwater levels due to the phenomenon of the rising Nile
Valley, whereby the siltation from the annual floodwaters of the
Nile continually raised the ground elevation of the lands and,
subsequently, groundwater levels.

Evidence remains, from many Ancient Egyptian texts, temples,
and tombs, which corroborates the accounts of the Greek and
Roman writers. For example, temples throughout Egypt make
reference to being originally built much earlier than their "dynas-
tic history". The texts inscribed in the crypts of the temple of
Hathor at Dendera clearly state that the temple that was restored
during the Ptolemaic Era was based on drawings dating back to
King Pepi of the 6th Dynasty (2400 BCE). The drawings themselves are copies of documents that are thousands of years older,
from the time of *Servants of Horus*. [Detailed and extensive elabo-
ration on this subject matter is found in the book *Ancient Egyptian Culture Revealed* by Moustafa Gadalla.]

9.2 THE MOST POPULOUS, RICHEST AND INFLUENTIAL

Egypt was the most dominant, populous, and famed country in the ancient world, as affirmed by Diodorus, *Book I*, [31, 6-9]:

> *"In density of population Egypt far surpassed of old all known regions of the inhabited world, and even in our own day is thought to be second to none . ."*

Superficially, Ancient Egypt seems isolated and distinct from the rest of the world, isolated by the deserts that hem in the narrow valley of the Nile. Yet, the Egyptians were in constant contact with other countries. Classical writers such as Plutarch, Herodotus, and Diodorus told how Ancient Egypt had peaceful colonies throughout the world. Diodorus of Sicily, in *Book I*, [29, 5], states:

> *"In general, the Egyptians say that their ancestors sent forth numerous colonies to many parts of the inhabited world, by reason of the pre-eminence of their former kings and their excessive population;"*

Diodorus, *Book I*, [28, 1-4], tells of some peaceful Egyptian colonies that were reported to him in Asia and Europe:

> *". . . a great number of colonies were spread from Egypt over all the inhabited world. To Babylon, for instance, colonists were led by Belus, who was held to be the son of Poseidon and Libya*
>
> *. . .*
>
> *. . . They say also that those who set forth with Danaus, like-wise from Egypt, settled what is practically the oldest city of Greece, Argos, and that the nation of the Colchi in Pontus and that of the Jews, which lies between Arabia and Syria, were founded as colonies by certain emigrants from their country. . ."*

By virtue of the eminence of the Egyptian colonists in Asia and Europe, they played a major role in the country of their new settlements. Diodorus, in *Book I*, [28,6-7], discusses the significant role of the Egyptian colonists as rulers of these new colonies.

Lastly, it should be noted that Ancient Egyptian records (as well as records in other areas) have countless names of places in the world that are not recognizable in our present time. Names of places, ethnic groups, and countries keep on changing. The names of European countries just 100 years ago, for example, are unrecognizable to most present-day Europeans. Eventually, when these records disappear a few centuries from now, the names of such countries will be totally unrecognizable.

In numerous locations in the world, there are references to tanned/brown-skinned people who provided enlightenment in regions throughout the world. They are described as:

1. Of "oriental" origin and characteristics.

2. Un-warlike people who settled peacefully among the local population.

3. Highly advanced in metallurgy, and have manufactured large quantities of metal products.

4. Highly organized and very talented in management.

5. Highly advanced in dry weather farming, irrigation, etc.

6. Experienced builders and artisans who have built megalithic tombs, etc.

7. Very religious people who had Animistic beliefs.

The above descriptions can only apply to one country—Egypt.

Immigration from Egypt occurred in several waves. It was

closely related to events in Ancient Egypt. Some left in prosperous times to pursue business contacts. The majority left in stressful times.

For more information about the Egyptian immigration waves to sub-Sahara and interior Africa, read *Exiled Egyptians: the Heart of Africa,* by Moustafa Gadalla.

For more information about the Egyptian immigration waves to the Iberian Peninsula, read *Egyptian Romany: the Essence of Hispania,* by Moustafa Gadalla.

SELECTED BIBLIOGRAPHY

Badawy, Alexander. *Ancient Egyptian Architectural Design*. Los Angeles, CA, USA, 1965.

Baines, John and Jaromir Málek. *Atlas of Ancient Egypt*. New York, 1994.

Budge, Sir E.A. Wallis. *Egyptian Language, Easy Lessons in Egyptian Hieroglyphics*. New York, 1983.
  - *The Gods of the Egyptians*, 2 volumes. New York, Dover, 1969.
  - *Osiris & The Egyptian Resurrection* (2 vols.). New York, 1973.

De Cenival, Jean-Louis. *Living Architecture*. Tr. by K.M. Leake. New York, 1964.

Diodorus of Sicily. *Books I, II, & IV*, tr. By C.H. Oldfather. London, 1964.

Egyptian Book of the Dead (*The Book of Going Forth by Day*), The Papyrus of Ani. USA, 1991.

Erman, Adolf. *Life in Ancient Egypt*. New York, 1971.

Erman, Adolf. *The Literature of the Ancient Egyptians*. Tr. By A.M. Blackman. London, 1927.

Gadalla, Moustafa.
  - See list of Publications at the end of this book.

Herodotus. *The Histories*, tr. A. de Selincourt. New York and Harmondsworth, 1954.

Iversen, Erik. *The Myth of Egypt & Its Hieroglyphs*. Copenhagen, 1961.

James, T.G.H. *An Introduction to Ancient Egypt*. London, 1979.

Kastor, Joseph. *Wings of the Falcon, Life and Thought of Ancient Egypt*. USA, 1968.

Piankoff, Alexandre. *The Litany of Re*. New York, 1964.
   – *The Pyramid of Unas Texts*. Princeton, NJ, USA, 1968.
   – *Mythological Papyri*. New York, 1957.
   – *The Shrines of Tut-Ankh-Amon Texts*. New York, 1955.

Plato. *The Collected Dialogues of Plato including the Letters*. Edited by E. Hamilton & H. Cairns. New York, USA, 1961.

Plotinus. *The Enneads*, in 6 Volumes, Tr. by A.H. Armstrong. London, 1978.

Plutarch. *Plutarch's Moralia*, Volume V. Tr. by Frank Cole Babbitt. London, 1927.

Strabo, *The Geography of Strabo*, Tr. By Jones, Horace Leonard. London, 1917.

Wilkinson, J. Gardner. *The Ancient Egyptians: Their Life and Customs*. London, 1988.